HEAT

T0362596

Series 3 Number 3

Caroline Rothwell
Museum 5 2015
Aquatint and blind embossing
Stencil drawn and cut on copper plate
by the artist, processed and printed
in an edition of fifteen

This work was produced as part of
the *Antipodes* project, a collaboration
between the Australian Print
Workshop, Melbourne, and the
Museum of Archaeology and
Anthropology, Cambridge, to study
rarely seen and highly significant
collections relating to Australia and
the Pacific and explore the interplay
of natural history, empire, art and
anthropology.

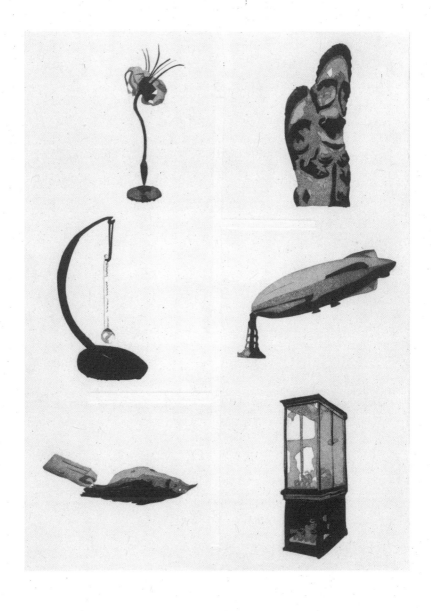

MADELEINE WATTS
AUSTRALIAN CAPITAL TERRITORY

Madeleine Watts is the author of the novel *The Inland Sea*, shortlisted for the 2021 Miles Franklin Literary Award. Her essays and short stories have been published in *Harper's*, *The White Review*, *The Believer* and *Griffith Review*, among others. She grew up in Sydney, and lives in New York.

WE WERE TRYING TO FIND SOMEWHERE in the city to have sex. It was three in the afternoon and we had been driving through the suburbs for two hours, looking for the right spot. For any spot. We were only visiting Canberra for two weeks. Neither of us had much of a sense of the city, of its layout or its secret places, no idea where might be best to drive towards. My phone was the only one with a functional SIM card, and so I used it to look at the digitised map. There were green stretches all over the capital. Green seemed useful. Green meant bushland. To the north lay the contours of Mount Ainslie and the Black Mountain Nature Reserve. They seemed practicable for our purposes, but we were starting from the south side of the city's artificial lake. On this side of the map I could see a long corridor of green, from the Federal Golf Club, to a lookout at Red Hill, and then, crossing a highway, Mugga Mugga Nature Reserve, and Isaacs Ridge. Let's head there, I said, investing hope in a place that was far from the National Gallery and the National Archives, from the High Court and the glassy low-rise government offices where everybody in the city seemed to spend their days. What kind of a city has so much green space, I asked from the passenger seat. Neel moved his left hand across the gear stick to my thigh and squeezed. It had been five and a half days. We were desperate.

We had woken early that morning. I had prepared breakfast in the kitchen and watched Neel crouching on the other side of the untidy dining table, coaxing his nephew out of a onesie and into trousers and jumper and socks. I had spooned unsweetened yogurt and mashed-up banana into the eighteen-month-old's mouth. We were in the car by half past seven. We drove across Lake Burley Griffin, along Northbourne Avenue with the raised

9

spectre of Parliament House looming over the bridge as we approached. I twisted around to speak to Neel's nephew in the backseat, pointed through the windscreen, and said, look, there it is. He glanced impassively towards the hill and then returned his attention to the velcro strap of his shoes. I turned to Neel and said, I guess that's the appropriate level of interest. He was just at the edge of babyhood, a nascent toddler. Soon he would be able to wreak havoc, tell secrets, attempt small escapes, but not yet.

We were in Canberra because Neel's sister-in-law had just delivered a second baby prematurely. While she recuperated, their first child needed tending, and we could help. We had driven the grim highway from Sydney to the capital, and had signed on for two weeks of care. And so we had become familiar with this early morning drive through the city. For those two weeks, we would sleep in the spare bedroom on a queen-sized bed that left space for little else in the room. The bedroom had big glass sliding doors looking out over a park behind the courtyard, behind which lay a mostly empty playground and the North Lyneham shopping centre – 'It's Happening!' The house was close to bushland, although everything in the city was close to bushland. The heating was turned off in the middle of the day to save money, and so we worked from bed under two duvets and a tartan picnic blanket. It was the start of cold and flu season, mornings of misted breath and dew in spider webs, dusks full of wood smoke, dog-walkers in fleeces and ugg boots. Neel's nephew, naturally, had a cold. We took a left before Parliament House, and drove through streets named for other Australian cities and states – Brisbane Avenue, New South Wales Crescent – to a nondescript four-storey glass building, behind which was the childcare centre where we were to deliver Neel's nephew. He sat in the back, strapped into his child seat, showing me his shoes while mucus streamed out of his nose. *Nase putzen,* I said to him, taking a tissue and scraping it under the toddler's nose, feeling the wet, gloopy strangeness of another person's snot between my fingers. The toddler was being brought up bilingual, and in the week we had spent helping to care for him, I had picked up these shreds of baby German. *Fertig,* I could ask when the toddler had stopped eating and wanted to clap his hands instead. *Hoppla,* I had learned to say when he tripped over. *Mehr* was his most commonly called-upon word. He was a child who always wanted more. He would bop up and down in his highchair and repeat the word like other children call for their mothers, never satisfied, wanting more penne, more raspberries, more olives, more brown bread and cream cheese. More, more, more.

Neel and I agreed that it was strange, indeed interesting, to be performing this kind of childcare; feeding and bathing and storying and bedding his nephew. As though in some way we were practising, seeing how we would do it ourselves. We should have a girl, we had said. She will have curly, black hair. We will read her Sherlock Holmes and *Paradise Lost*. We will do it differently. Every morning I was careful to take the pill at precisely nine o'clock, and sometimes Neel would check, to reassure himself that I had. But there was a fizzy sensation to these jokes and assurances. A way of saying, without quite saying it, that although this was new we were in it for the long haul. Do you want to marry him, my mother had asked after meeting Neel. I had shrugged. Who knows. You two should get a dog, Neel's father advised. He advised because we had both, after a decade living variously in America and England and Spain and Vietnam, decided at last to move back. A month earlier we had signed the lease on a cold house in the Blue Mountains, west of Sydney. On that day in Canberra we had been together thirteen months. Steady, happy months. We owned Ikea furniture together, had combined our books, were joint owners of a Turkish kilim, a record player, and a vibrator. Maybe we would start gardening. Maybe we would get a dog. Maybe we would have a baby, a girl, with curly, black hair.

In Canberra we had taken to listening to a community radio station when we were in the car. ArtSound FM played jazz, folk and 'world music'. They hosted a program called the Bach Hour, another called the Tiki Lounge Remix, and the Hit Parade of Yesterday played Ma Rainey, Gracie Fields, and Duke Ellington. We had become fond of the people we imagined ran the station: muddled public servants, Birkenstock wearers, well-meaning retirees like our parents. Even the radio station had a part to play in the reassuring pantomime of that week, when the toddler was in the backseat, when we could pass for his parents. Imagine a life like this, we play-acted to one another: a life where we drive a fifteen-year-old maroon Toyota with an old FM scanner, where we listen to this radio station all the time, and are happy.

Neel's nephew safely deposited at the day care centre, we had the whole afternoon ahead of us. And so we drove up to Red Hill Nature Reserve to the sounds of late-period Miles Davis. But there were teenagers picnicking on the crest of the lookout, and the golf club was bigger than we thought. Neel drove, and I searched the map. He kept his hand on my thigh, one finger stroking the fabric of my skirt. I moved my hand to the back of his neck and held on. I loved that neck, that skin. He was the first man who had ever asked me to look him in the eye when we were fucking. It had flustered me, when he pointed it out, when he asked me to look at him, the very first time we went to bed together. On the sofa, actually. With a lamp on in the corner, at two in the morning after many hours of separately sitting together in my living room, just talking, too timid to move closer to one another across the vast expanse of the room. Not until he asked me to get up from the floor and come and sit beside him on the sofa, please. That had been the tipping point, that evening thirteen months ago in New York. The clothes shredded, skin wet and soft on a rough blanket, the rising tide of orgasm, and then the shock of another, and another. Meeting his eyes while I came, a kind of unravelling of the thread that had kept me bound. He had unravelled everything I thought I knew about my life, proposed by his very presence a happiness I thought I would never deserve. Now, in the car, it was difficult to keep from looking at him, to stop myself from touching the soft black hair that grew along his cheeks above his beard. From leaning over the gear stick to lick his throat. We kept driving south towards the green spaces on the map. We wanted a long trail road. Somewhere difficult to find.

We drove through the green corridor of Mugga Mugga Nature Reserve, past an animal shelter, a Murray's coach depot, and an asphalt quarry that engulfed the car in a dark, viscous smell. But there were no turn-offs in sight. I could see trails on the map on my phone, which corresponded to the stretch of bush we passed through, but we could not see entrances to any of the trails. We drove up Long Gully Road, and then back again, before I spotted one.

Shall we? he asked me. I assented.

We parked on loose gravel, at the entrance to a track shut to cars by a yellow gate. Behind the gate a walkable path veered into the trees. Along the ridge to the left of Long Gully Road grew a steep slope of box gum, but beyond and rising above the gums were the high peaks of a pine plantation. The pines were tall. We could almost imagine we were in the northern hemisphere. To the south of the road we could see what I would later learn was the Brindabella Range, when I looked at the map on my phone as we drove back towards Parliament House. *There*, I thought, touching the green space on the map with my index finger and thumb.

We had both been to Canberra before, separately, and long ago. Neel had visited once, after his brother and sister-in-law relocated, and for two years when I was a teenager my father had lived here. He had taken a job in one of the country's government departments, and I had visited him three times. I hated it. Go for a walk, my father would insist then, it isn't healthy for a sixteen-year-old to be in the house all day. I countered that there was nothing to do in Canberra, nothing to satisfy a sixteen-year-old, at least. To mollify my father, I would go off on walks into the bushland behind his house, listening to maudlin British music from the 1980s that did not match the vista of rough buff-green scrub and sandy soil and miles and miles of nothingness. Those were drought years. Fires burned every summer. A few months before my father moved to Canberra, fires had burned the Mount Stromlo Observatory, the Water Quality Control Centre, and many houses. Four people burned alive. Nothing grew, and by the sides of the roads the grass had turned to yellow tinder. But the fields were still full of kangaroos, even then, regardless of the drought. Large families grazed by freeways, on grass verges, in the bushes growing on the median strips. They were known to jump in front of cars. During those years international animal rights groups were accusing the Australian government of animal cruelty. The government, my father told me, would imminently institute a large-scale kangaroo cull in the capital. The animals dented drivers' bumpers and smashed windshields. The sides of the roads were littered with kangaroo corpses, and that looked bad to visiting dignitaries. They were pests, like rabbits, my father had said, and the animal rights groups overseas, which thought the kangaroos were cuddly, special, and worthy of protection, didn't know what they were talking about. The cull was carried out, huge numbers of animals shot, but fifteen years later the kangaroos were as prevalent as I remembered. We had seen them in far paddocks, grazing, or in bushland, reclining like Manet's *Olympia*.

We had been excited at first – neither of us had seen kangaroos in so long – and we viewed them for a time as though we were foreigners ourselves. But we soon re-adjusted. They became commonplace. On many roads all over Canberra there were warning signs, a black illustration of a hopping kangaroo on a white rectangle, with the warning that we were entering a 'High Incident' area. We had not hit one. But we had seen their bodies, the soft brown carcasses. Human-sized. Had seen the flesh shrinking around the teeth in their tightening skulls, and a wound where the red and pink atrocity of organs spilled out of their bodies and into the dirt on the sides of four-lane roads. *Check the pouch,* I thought, every time we passed one on the roads. The idea of something small, suddenly unmothered, made my toes clench, made my stomach turn. But we never stopped the car to see if there was a joey still alive in the wreckage of the roadside kangaroos, or what was left of them. Kept driving.

We took our affections where we could. We had bought the Sydney newspaper from a newsagent in Manuka and done the crossword together, sitting side by side on a concrete bench looking onto a children's karate school. We had made a trip to Big W and held hands as we waited by the loading dock to collect the package of baby supplies Neel's sister-in-law had ordered. We had embraced in the pharmaceutical aisle of the Coles at Jamison Centre, Macquarie. We hugged in the kitchen while we prepared porridge and toast and pasta for the toddler, and I got up on my tiptoes to press my pelvis into Neel's. You poor thing, Neel whispered in my ear, holding me in such a way that his hands grazed the sides of my breasts. I was shocked, in those moments, at how I responded. How like an animal I was discovering myself to be: insistent, carnal, and vulnerable. I had never felt so close to instinct, pheromones, physicality, as I did in those moments that I wanted Neel. And then his nephew would appear, with a toy he wanted, or on the way to a forbidden drawer he wished to open, or more often, seeing some food, and asking for more. *Mehr,* he would say, and I would reach for what he wanted. In this way we looked after Neel's nephew, while his brother worked and his sister-in-law cared for her newest-born, and we did not mind. His brother worked late into the night, his sister-in-law was constantly expressing milk. The time they spent together they sat in the dimmed living room, watching American films dubbed into German, English subtitles stuttering across the screen. This, Neel commented, was the kind of exhaustion we were in for. A bone-sapping tiredness, wordlessness, a going-to-bed-at-nine o'clock life.

I'll take it, I thought. I wanted that wordless place. I longed for the bone-sapping tiredness.

I'm sorry to have brought you to this weird place, to do these weird things with me, Neel said, kneeling on a foam mat printed with the primary coloured aerial view of train tracks, wiping the shit from his nephew's bottom. It's okay, I replied, trying to extricate the Cruskit from his nephew's mouth while he was lying flat on his back, a choking hazard, I tried to reason with the toddler, *alles gut*, just spit it out, not knowing the German for it. Really, it's okay. I'm having a lovely time.

A week earlier we had arrived, and on that first evening in the city we were thrown full-force into childcare. The parents were still at the hospital, the newborn had jaundice, Neel's sister-in-law had elevated blood pressure. We were on our own. We drove in the darkness down Brisbane Avenue to the childcare centre. Neel had to be added to the secure caretaker list, to allow us to pick up his nephew, and for five minutes we stood at the gate while he fumbled with the security system, the pin he had to enter, the two-factor authentication that didn't work, and all the while the children played on the astroturf over the fence, paying us no attention. His nephew was ushered to the gate, beaming, holding a half-masticated rice cake in his hand, and continued to beam until he saw that we were not familiar. He burst into tears. I picked him up and he sobbed into my shoulder as we opened the door and placed him in the car seat. Neel fumbled with the straps. Neither of us knew how to work a car seat. His nephew continued to sob until I reached a hand around Neel and patted the child's round belly. I was wearing two red bangles, which clacked pleasingly against one another. The toddler grasped them, tried the clacking out for himself. The crying stopped. His small fingers stroked my fingernails, where my red nail polish had just begun to chip. He beamed. We drove back to Neel's brothers house, not precisely sure what we were meant to do when we arrived. For the first fifteen minutes we watched the toddler play on the floor of the living room. Should we take his shoes off, I wondered. What if he cries, asked Neel. We stood side by side in the doorway, as though we might be able to leave. But then Neel's phone rang, and he bent down, sat with his nephew on the floor and talked to his sister-in-law over FaceTime. He angled the phone's screen towards the child, who was instructed to be good, in German. In the kitchen I put pellets of frozen spinach and jarred pesto and microwaved ravioli into a food processor, and blitzed it to a green paste. *Mehr,* the child said, bopping in his seat when it was all eaten. We proffered cheese, a mandarin, some olives, but still he wanted more. He threw his plastic bottle of water from the highchair to the ground, then wailed when it was out of reach. Neel retrieved it, handed it back. He dropped it again. Wailed. Each time he seemed to experience a deep, overwhelming grief at the loss of his bottle, and yet the memory of the grief did not stop him from replicating the emotional experience again and again, so satisfying was the thud of the loss. When we heaved him out of the chair his face and hands were covered in green smears, in mandarin juice, in the thick oil from marinated olives. Upstairs in the bathroom Neel carefully undressed him. My mum said he was hairy, Neel said to me, and she wasn't wrong. He pointed out the dark hair growing between the child's butt cheeks, and once he was in the bath we could see the same dark hairs growing all over his back. We dunked warm water over him, scrubbed his back, while the child played with plastic toys that variously spouted, streamed or sprayed water. Do we need to clean his bottom, I asked. We both knelt on the bathroom tiles peering over the side of the bathtub at the child, unsure. Maybe just being in the water is enough? The boy was kneeling in the bath, transfixed by what he had discovered he could do with his legs. Bringing his thighs together and then apart, he watched his penis disappear and reappear. We watched with him, for a few moments. The concealing and revealing. It starts so early, I observed. We dried him in a large towel so that he wouldn't feel the biting cold of the all-day unheated house, and let him walk down the corridor to his bedroom, past the childproof gate at the top of the staircase. Neel laid him on the floor and attempted to dress him. His hands got stuck in the arms of his pyjamas, and the child wailed. Please don't cry, Neel said, *alles gut, ja, alles gut,* and when the ordeal was over the child turned to me and put his arms around my neck, burying his face in my shoulder. I had not experienced a feeling quite like the one I had then, a feeling of deep satisfaction, of tenderness, calm. The surge of dopamine, drug-like and tingly, from his soft, clean skin and the warmth of his head. I want this, I thought. My whole body throbbed with it. I did not tell Neel what I was feeling, but I sat the baby in my lap and held onto him, kissing the top of his head where it smelled so good. I read to him from the books in the room, letting him pick by pointing. The story he chose was

19

about a little girl who gets lost in the bush. It was a board book version of an old classic, one that looked like a hand-me-down from parents of an older child. I knew it – I had grown up reading about the same little girl in the bush. The child put his finger on the picture of the kangaroo and the little girl snug within her pouch. *Mehr,* he said, and bounced in my lap. *Nein,* I replied, it's time to sleep. Half past seven, we had been told, put him in the crib, turn the lights out, close the door, don't look back. No hugs, no kisses goodnight. He will cry, but it should stop after ten minutes.

From the bottom of the staircase we listened to the weeping. Neel put his arms around me and we stood there, tense, every wail ripping through us. After eight minutes the crying stopped. There was silence. The house was ours. We returned to the kitchen and I poured large glasses of red wine for us both, but Neel reached across the kitchen counter and pulled me into him. His hand on my breast, my hand on his belt buckle. We hurried as quietly as we could up the squeaking staircase to the spare bedroom, closed the curtains over the sliding glass door, and turned on the lamp. The room lit up with soft light. I sunk into the two duvets and opened my legs. Neel did not wait to undress me. It was all too urgent. But I had trouble keeping quiet. Shhh, Neel said, be careful. But as hard as I tried, I could not stop myself from crying out. My noises woke the toddler. We both struggled to orgasm through the sobbing penetrating the shared wall. Neel pulled his trousers up, I pulled my skirt down, and we opened the door to the bedroom where the child was standing in his crib, holding onto the railings, red-faced and still sobbing. I took him in my arms and rocked him. Neel stood beside me, rubbing my shoulder. We both knew we would need to find somewhere else, we couldn't have sex in the house.

Cars sped by on Long Gully Road, and a breeze rustled the leaves of the box gums lining the ridge. We had a couple of hours, we thought, but no more. I had a fleece-lined denim jacket that I pulled tight around me, although it was not especially cold. Neel locked the car. We hoped our things would be safe. He put his arm around me, and I nestled my head against his shoulder. Entwined, we ascended the hill, in our matching boots, which he had polished for us the night before in his brother's lounge room in Lyneham while I lay on the grey imitation-leather sofa and read to him from a book about whale song.

From the gravel path we passed beyond the yellow gate and left the sound of the cars behind us. Brown metal signs were nailed to trees along the path, ornamented with insignias of riders, arrows pointing the way. The path ascended steeply ahead of us. He kept his arm tight around my shoulders, where he could bend down, occasionally, to kiss the skin on my temples. I could feel parts of my body begin to tense and light up. A tightness in my stomach, a catching of breath, an anticipation felt in the hardening of my nipples, in the tensing of the muscles of my thighs. We ascended the steep ridge, beginning to pant, with the afternoon sun tending to a deeper orange, west through the pines. At that time of year, the sun set at five in the afternoon. We had only an hour and a half left, I thought, of light.

It was hard to tell how high we had climbed, but we were winded. The sounds of the cars were faint. Ghosts of mountain bikes had beaten up mud that had dried into humps along the trail. We began to look for anywhere flat enough to lie down, a place where the steep slope might level out. We seemed to be the sole inhabitants of the pines. What about those rocks, Neel said, pointing uphill. The ridge above looked treacherous. Stone boulders were interspersed with ironbarks, acacia scrub and stunted tea trees, a slope of deathbed colours rising up and pulling down. Come on, he said.

I followed him. Our boots sunk into the leaf litter. I kept my eyes on my feet, on small holes in the dirt that might have been burrows, on the uneven ground, trying to step where he had stepped. I looked upwards, occasionally, trying to discern where he was taking us. The tall slope of his body, the blue jumper and long, black denim legs.

When I was little, it was my father who had read me the book about the little girl and the kangaroo bounding through the bush, the longer version of the board book I had read to Neel's nephew. In the long version, the story began with a little girl crying, alone and frightened, when a motherly kangaroo hopped by and offered her help. The kangaroo fed her berries, which gave the little girl the ability to understand the language of the animals. Suddenly the bush was alive with chatter. It turned out that the kangaroo had suffered a loss of her own. Hunted by humans one day, she had not long ago lost her joey. So the kangaroo put the little girl in her pouch, and off they bounded into the bush. The story suggested that the trauma of the loss was erased when the kangaroo found the little girl and tended to her. But the kangaroo's loss of her joey upset me. Why, I had wondered then, was there need of a hunt? The book told a story where humans learn to recognise they are just one part of the ecology of the bush, no more important than the platypus or the wombat or the kookaburra, but no less valuable either. In the end the little girl's family creates a waterhole, and the animals of the bush move unimpeded across the property. Coexistence. But I knew even as a child that was not the case in the wide world, knew that the bush was full of horse riders and mountain bikers and dead kangaroos on the sides of the road. The pine forest at Isaacs Ridge where Neel and I were walking was in the middle of suburban sprawl. In the winter, the national park still sent contract shooters into the reserve to cull the kangaroos. They used silencers on the guns, so as not to alert the nearby residents to the slaughter. As Neel led us up the hill, the only sign of other people were the cartridges left behind by the hunters, half buried in the dust and the scrub.

When Neel decided on a rock we were so high above the path we had left we could not see it anymore through the trees. Is this alright? he asked. I kissed him. He made to sit down on the rock, but I stopped him. Hang on. I took my jacket off. I found a stick laying nearby, picked it up, and scraped off the surface of the nearly flat granite, all the dust and pellets of kangaroo shit, as dry and as round as peppercorns. When it was clean enough I lay my jacket across the rock. He grinned, and sat down. He put his hands on my waist and drew me into his legs. My heels dug into the dirt to steady me on the steep slope. His hand went to my hip, and then began to bunch and pull up the fabric of my long skirt. Hang on, I said again. I lifted my left leg, and pulled off my boot. I balanced, my hand on his shoulder, and reached beneath my skirt to roll my winter tights and underwear down. When the tights were low enough I unrolled them over my foot, and put the boot back on. Then I switched legs, and repeated the action. I rolled the tights and underwear into a ball and placed them beside Neel. I could feel the breeze through my skirt, the way it insinuated itself between my legs. He drew me in. His hand went under my skirt. He touched me between my legs, felt what was already wet. Baby, he said, as though it were a gift. He began to stroke me.

He pushed me off his lap and turned me. He sat me down on the jacket, and knelt. The late afternoon light overcame us. He parted my legs and pushed my skirt up to my waist. My feet did not quite touch the ground below, but my toes and the balls of my feet could feel the earth. I pressed down through my boots, to keep my body steady. He knelt. In the light the skin of my legs and pubic bone were incredibly pale, an almost sickly white. I could see the speckles of dark hair threatening to regrow from the previous night's shaving, and the ghosts of stretch marks running perpendicularly along my inner thighs. Down there on his knees, he examined me. There was a vulnerability to that gaze, all the imperfectability of my body there in front of him, for him to reject or desire as he found fit. He clasped his hands around my thighs, very gently, and then leant forward. I could smell the sweet odour of shit from somewhere behind me. He kissed the wet lips of my labia. Then he began to lick me. I opened my eyes and looked up, to the brilliant sky and the towering pines and all that light. The ranges, brown and surging through the trees.

He had been using the flat of his tongue against me, but now began to use the tip, flicking it back and forth with greater frequency across my clitoris, intensifying the pleasure in the way he had learned. I want to be able to play you like an instrument, he had written to me once, in the beginning of our courtship. It was the kind of cliché that had taken on a life outside itself and formed a peculiar and particular resonance between the two of us, because thirteen months later, he could. The trembling began, the tension in my thighs from keeping my body balanced on the rock caused my legs to quiver, my forearms tense. The orgasm began to shake me, and as my ragged breaths and cries and shouts rang out, even though I loved him, I did not look at him at all. I came to the sight of pines and light and mountains, towards the forest.

He stood up, bent down, and kissed me. The viscous mess of me was smeared through his beard, catching the light. I caught the taste of myself on his tongue. I stood up, so he could sit. I unzipped his trousers, and he helped pull down his underwear. I shuffled forward through the leaf litter towards his groin. I hoisted my right knee onto the rock beside him, but there was not room enough on the left, and so I kept it balanced on the earth below. When I was in his lap he held me tight. It occurred to me that if he were to let go and I was not prepared, I would go tumbling straight down the ridge, to that yellow sandy path we had abandoned below. He used his hand to manoeuvre himself inside me. We were forced to be slow, and this slowness made it difficult, more awkward somehow. It feels so good to be inside you, he said, his mouth at my collarbone. The movement was difficult, with muscles tensed to balance me, and one leg on a rock, and the fear of the fall if he loosened his grip. Gentle, he said, but I was not good at being gentle. I bit into his shoulder, feeling flesh beneath the wool and flannel caught between my teeth. I knew that over my shoulder he could see all that light, those pines, those mountains. I listened to him come, to both of our cries, echoing out all over the ridge.

As we stepped carefully through the rocks and scrub in the direction of the path and the car, Neel stopped me and pointed downhill. Is that a kangaroo? he asked. I focused, and eventually saw the brown shape through the trees. It's quite small, I said. It might be a wallaby. Neither of us knew the difference, only that wallabies were smaller than kangaroos.

It twitched, and then the kangaroo stood perfectly still. We made eye contact with the animal. It seemed to recognise us for what we were. It sensed the blood pumping through our veins, and the grilled fish from the Canberra Southern Cross Club digesting in our stomachs and the persistent pheromonal yearning legible in the scent of our sweat. The kangaroo saw us for other animals, I believed. Then it turned. We watched it hop downhill, and out of sight, into the dense thicket of pines. A gust of wind rolling down off the Snowy Mountains sent the pines creaking like they were about to fall down. I expected the sound of a shot, some sign of a hunter. But no shots came, and the animal was gone, vanished into the same pines that had sheltered us. I think there was a joey in its pouch, I said to Neel, although I wasn't sure. I really didn't know.

Half an hour later the sun was gone. We drove to Coles in Manuka and parked underground. We bought red peppers and chickpeas for a salad. We bought bottles of Fiji water because they were on special, and a packet of caramel slices, because we were ravenous.

Beneath my long skirt I still had no tights or underwear, and the tops of my thighs were wet and slippery where they touched. With my liquids, with his. My denim jacket looked clean from the outside, but the fleece beneath was specked with dust and twigs and kangaroo shit. We stood entwined on the escalator, kissing, obstructing foot traffic. We paid scant attention to the barber, the TAB, the shuttered Flight Centre, the harried public servants buying something quick for dinner on the way home. We were happy. The radio was full of smooth jazz and sitars. We drove through the deserted civic streets to collect his nephew, whose nose was running terribly, who coughed all the way home, whose face I wiped, and who I let hold my bangles because he liked the colours and the sound they made. *Nase putzen*, I said to him, and he showed me, once more, his shoes. We drove north together, the three of us, across Lake Burley Griffin in the dark, over that bridge whose name I never learned and the dark still waters away from Parliament House.

KENNETH CHONG
SMALL TALK

Kenneth Chong is a writer based in Sydney. His fiction, essays and reviews have appeared in publications such as *Books & Culture* and *Add to Cart Magazine*, where he is also an editor. He graduated from Princeton University with a doctorate in English, and is at work on a novel and an opera libretto.

AS A MAN WRITES THIS DOWN, he calls to mind those many instances in which he wished he was at home, reading. He would say to himself, I wish I were at home now, and then picture himself huddled up with a book of no particular title, but nevertheless certain that the pleasure and comfort he found in that imagined tableau would exceed anything before his eyes. Usually what he saw, in what others would call real life, was a party gathering of young people, who were awkwardly seated in ill-fitting suits and brightly coloured dresses, learning how to eat with the right set of forks and knives, and how to empty a glass by tilting its stem. At a certain point, when the characters on stage had stopped their speeches and food was in abeyance, the lights would dim and some music that the man recognised as the sort he heard while wandering through shopping malls would play at high volume; soon there would be several out on the dance floor, and reluctant partners (mostly male) would follow. But the man would remain in his seat and look on at the circle forming around one or another dancer, or notice how the strobes coloured a bridesmaid's magenta dress, or how the roaming spotlight might chance upon a foot or an ear, a high heel lifted or a ribbon askew. The man would never dance, even if others around him forced the heavy-footed onto the dance floor. He would get on his feet only to walk to the bathroom, where he would take his time urinating and washing and drying his hands and slowly making his way back, mesmerised by the moving colours of the light. And then he would sit down again, wait for dessert, and distract himself with anything that might take attention from dancing, all the while thinking: I would rather be at home, reading.

It was not that the man was antisocial. As a child of migrants who lived in the suburbs of the North or Northwest of Sydney, he had grown up under much the same conditions as many of these wedding guests. He could be described as reserved and quiet, but was friendly enough to engage in some 'small talk'. He had come to learn from his pastor – the young but grey-haired minister of an English-speaking congregation at a Chinese church, as it was called – that small talk was an invaluable thing to engage in. To be sure, small talk was just chitchat, of little relevance in the larger scheme of things, but without small talk it would be impossible to talk about deeper things. Perhaps it should have been called shallow talk, implying that there was by contrast deep talk, but the man had never heard that term. It was small talk. And so the man tried as best as he could, remembering what his pastor had told him, to be a good small talker.

One thing the pastor had suggested was never to ask what the person with whom one was having small talk did for a living. One should avoid at all costs embarrassing the person, should the reluctant answer be that the person did not work, or that the person was a labourer or a receptionist or did something not particularly reputable. Of course, there would be some who would wish to volunteer such information, having in their possession a title or occupation of some esteem (a doctor, a lawyer, an accountant) or being in the process of acquiring it. But for the most part it was better, the pastor had advised, to begin the conversation elsewhere rather than, in his words, put them immediately in a box, a category or type of person one could confidently name – and so bring the conversation to an abrupt halt. The other reason, the pastor had said, was that one wished to withhold judgment, to resist defining a person by a job currently held, which in all likelihood the person had learned to identify with and lean upon in times of doubt and crisis, but which could easily be the cause of doubt and crisis in the person's so-called identity, tied up as it was with the person's function in everyday society.

In practice, avoiding the question of a person's work was difficult. If one conscientiously avoided the subject, it became the absent centre around which all other talk revolved; if it were something that the interlocutor desired to answer, wishing to disclose it at any moment, there were only so many ways to avoid the topic or shift the conversation onto a plain where it was far from sight. But on occasion a shift was made, and the man and the interlocutor would enjoy a conversation free from the cultural imperative of needing to work or preparing to work, finding a landscape where the question of job and career was invisible, at best irrelevant. In these attempts at small talk, the man (who was at the time a young man) was stumbling with the interlocutor onto a field they had once glimpsed, but which had receded so much from view that they had hardly looked that way and, as they grew older, had begun to doubt its existence.

The young man had been confident that he might find it, or something close to it, in the church. This did not mean that he thought of the church, whether the red-brick Gothic building with two sandstone towers in the suburb of Milsons Point or the gatherings of people who met there or the various ministries that were in some way connected to it, as that once-glimpsed field, but there was something in it, what he might have termed truth or the Gospel or even love, which had led him to believe. The young man did not remember when he first believed, or whether there was a specific day and time when it could be said that he had crossed from darkness into light. He only remembers that he had found a dark blue playing-sized card between the pages of his blue leather *Student Bible,* edited by the American author Philip Yancey. After he had read from one or another chapter and verse from the Bible, he had looked at the dark blue card and saw a prayer in a cursive font, and decided to recite the words of the prayer as his own. He did this, saying the formulaic phrases under his breath, trying to show a certain seriousness as he uttered them – Dear God, I acknowledge I am a sinner... – in the hope that some decisive feeling of change might overcome him as he asked for forgiveness, thanked Jesus for dying on the cross, and presented himself as a newborn supplicant who was assured of God's approval, once and for all.

The problem, however, was that this was not the first time the young man had prayed this kind of prayer. He does not remember clearly any earlier time when he discovered a similar prayer card in his Bible which had prompted him to deliver himself, at least verbally, into the Saviour's arms. As a boy, the young man had attended one or two or three so-called evangelistic meetings. He had travelled in a midnight-blue Holden Berlina with his parents or an uncle and an auntie across the Sydney Harbour Bridge to sit in a large theatre on a Saturday evening. At the end of a rousing and energetic talk, which was the centrepiece of such meetings, the male speaker would call upon whoever felt led to lay their lives down for Jesus at the altar to do so now, and the boy would see several young women walk in the direction of the stage, first one, then another, and as others gathered courage (he surmised) several more. He would see the backs of the kneeling and standing figures, heads bowed, and after the speaker had laid an anointing hand on one or two of the heads and committed the newly faithful to God, the boy would catch a young woman's delicate pale face, half-reddened by tears, as she walked back to her seat. The boy was too young to understand what had been uttered by the speaker to this large group of mostly black-haired people, let alone to feel the compunction that had led some to approach the altar at the speaker's behest. He would learn that this was known as an altar call, although there was in reality no altar, just a brightly lit stage that was slightly elevated above the crowd. Nevertheless, he had wondered at the time what strange force had compelled these young women, who were probably in their early twenties, to decide in a single night to commit their lives to God and Jesus, to these characters who were mere strangers yesterday. What had overcome them to be so bold as to step forward, away from the crowd?

To the boy, God and Jesus were not strangers but familiar characters whom he addressed fairly regularly if not, at times, a little frivolously. When he prayed to God, he had once seen in his mind an old man with a grey beard, but a Sunday school teacher, whom he addressed by prefacing the teacher's first name with *auntie* even though they were not related, had said that that was not what God looked like. So the boy tried to shut out any image of God when the word *God* was mentioned, and imagined God closer to a voice which spoke from the clouds or out of the dark of night. But no one said to him that he could not imagine Jesus as a man with golden flowing hair, with blue eyes that looked on sympathetically at shepherds and their sheep and mysteriously cloaked women. When the boy was quite small, the image of Jesus in his mind was almost cartoonish, not so much coloured as whited out, leaving the mere outlines – as he had seen them in an illustrated Bible series for young children. Since the boy had never coloured in any of these outlined shapes, unlike other children of his age, the Jesus of his mind remained colourless, although at times, under the influence of other imagery and illustrations from his Sunday-school material, his Jesus would acquire golden locks or blue eyes or sometimes a light-brown beard. In most cases, coloured-in or not, his Jesus wore a white robe, which was secured by a thin black or brown belt and with always the right amount of folds.

God and Jesus did not seem to occupy the same reality plane as his parents and brother did. The boy had never been smacked by God, nor wrestled to the ground, nor forced to hold his breath under a pillow. Still, his parents spoke of God and Jesus in serious tones, and the boy assumed that the God and Jesus they spoke of was the God and Jesus he regularly addressed at night and before mealtimes. The young man had to admit that his saying grace, as it was called, was little more than perfunctory. In his defence, no matter how quickly he raced through the prayer – a prayer of two rhyming couplets he assumed he learned from his parents – he always said it before putting any meal to his lips (morning tea and snacks did not count). As a grown man he had discovered, to his surprise, that he could no longer recall all of the words. He was only certain that it contained the final lines, 'Thank you for the food we eat, / Thank you God for everything.'

But what did the boy pray when left to his own devices? His Sunday-school teachers had given him some direction, in the way they themselves prayed in class and, as he got older, in explicit guidelines as to how he might structure his so-called spontaneous prayers. If the boy was addressing God and uttering words inwardly so that they resonated somehow in the chamber of his heart, wasn't that a prayer of some sort? And if not exactly a prayer, at least the antithesis of small talk? But then, wasn't prayer in essence the antithesis of small talk?

The young man remembers that as a boy he would confide in God things he would never mention to his family or even his closest friends. At the onset of puberty, or slightly before, the boy rubbed himself while on a pine three-seater with olive-coloured cushions in the television room. The boy did not know why he had this sudden urge (the 68 cm television was off), or why after rubbing he felt oddly sated, but when his father walked into the room he quickly stood up and scampered to his room. Luckily, no traces were to be found. The young man remembers that later in the night, or in the nights that followed, the boy had confessed to God about what he called his *dickies*, which is the term he used until he learnt some years later in a biological textbook that it already had a conventional name. (The textbook had described the act as accompanied by a 'tingling sensation', something he pointed out to a male classmate in a mocking way. The classmate threatened to call him an epithet based on the name of the act; so the boy, who was by then a teenager, never mentioned anything to do with it at the all-boys school in North Sydney he attended for the remaining four years.) The boy was not sure whether what he had done was a sin or not, only that it was something he ought not to do in the television room but in the privacy of his own bedroom, or when no one was around. The young man remembers the boy had begun confessing this action of his, yet in the middle of confessing he had been puzzled about its apparent wrongness. The boy apologised all the same; God would not fault him for being overly cautious.

As the boy grew into a young man, he would find himself semi-confessing this sin, which he was still unsure as to whether it was a sin or not. By the time he started having squeaks in his voice, he knew that sexual intercourse outside of marriage was a grave and serious sin – as grave and serious as divorce. His parents never spoke of these things except cryptically or in passing, always a little embarrassed or (in the case of his father) unusually strident when the subject was broached. In Sunday school he had learned from balding men that to look at a woman lustfully was a sin, and according to Jesus was tantamount to committing adultery. But what was it to look at a woman lustfully? The boy who was now a teenager did not really know. He knew that when he saw pretty women in underwear, or when one of these women had her bra undone to reveal her breasts, he would regularly feel much the same urge as he did on the pine three-seater and abscond to his room if he could. As he lay on his bed he would close his eyes and try to conjure up an image in his mind of the image he had just seen in a Grace Bros catalogue or on television. But the image would not stay in his mind's eye for long – it would flicker or morph and, as his urgency arose, fade to nothing except for a few blotches.

The teenager always felt guilty after relieving his urges, but he was confused about his feeling so. He confessed it as a sin to God of course, but in his tangential prayers he would ask God, if such a line of questioning be allowed, what was precisely wrong with these acts of his. He had understood that he should flee from lust as the Bible commanded, but was the image of an attractive woman, which brought on certain urges which needed to be relieved, the same as adultery? The images that the teenager tried to bring to mind were not like any of those images of couples on television who were engaged, as the TV guide put it, in sex scenes. None of the images in his mind ever had a couple, even if the images of foreplay or sexual activity that he had seen on television usually involved a couple. He never imagined doing any of the things the male of the couple had done to the female of the couple, or rather he had only wished to gaze on the female in his mind as the male had done from where the male of the couple was sometimes positioned.

The teenager, however, had learnt not to speak of it, and in the rare or veiled instances that it came up he understood that it was an uncomfortable subject for adults and surely sinful. Yet while the act was denounced in the devotionals his father had given him to read daily, but which he never did for more than a stretch of a week, the various preachers who came to speak at church never denounced it outright and on occasion questioned the viewpoint of the devotional authors. The sin of onanism, one preacher had said, when he came across the Old Testament passage in his sermon and had no choice but to expound it, was not the sin of lust or self-pleasure, as some American commentators were wont to say, but the sin of pride: Onan, in spilling his seed on the ground when he slept with his brother's wife, was refusing to do his duty of giving his deceased brother an heir. If one were to condemn self-pleasure or self-love, as secular sources referred to it, one would have to go elsewhere in the Bible for support. But the teenager knew that would lead to all those passages in the New Testament that spoke of lust and adultery and divorce and remarriage, and so leave aside the burning question of what he had thought was the sin of onanism.

Only at a certain point, when the teenager was well on his way to becoming a young man, did he accept, without being entirely satisfied by any one reason, that the private acts he did in his bedroom or when no one was around were sinful, and that he wished for God to take away his desires if it were His will. He had been given the idea from a letter that had been addressed to the author of a devotional book, a letter from a young man from America who was writing this letter in order to avoid the sin he would be committing at the time of writing, which was presumably at night. The teenager who was almost a young man does not remember how the author of the devotional responded, but it was clear that the desires that tormented the teenager were also the desires that tormented the young man from America. It was a struggle, to use a word common among Christians, that would not go away anytime soon. The teenager thought that the struggle would stop or abate somewhat when he got married, but when he had become an adult in the eyes of the state he had read a book by another American author that said that marriage would not resolve the problem. The desires would remain, and when there was no wife to satisfy them a husband would be left to the devices he had when he was single. In this book (the front cover of which had the words *Pure Desire* in bold italics and a picture of two hands upturned as if receiving water from a fountain), the author had also asserted that being left to one's own devices meant one was always in the thrall of sin. It was impossible, the author said, for a man to relieve himself without the aid of what he called fantasy – and therefore without an image of a naked woman. The author himself gave a detailed account of his own fantasy-processes in which the unveiling of an image of a woman's vagina was necessary to bring him to climax, although he admitted that other (Christian) men he knew found other images of women or women's parts more necessary. Whatever the exact image or sequence of images required for men to relieve themselves, these images involved a certain unreality which turned women into objects.

The young man who was an adult was struck by the candour of the author, whose fantasy processes seemed to be similar to his own. At the time, the young man had continued to watch foreign movies late at night on the SBS TV channel in the hope of seeing an image of a woman which might bring about some sort of arousal, but he also waited for images of naked women to load onto the computer screen. The young man would click on a thumbnail image he wished to see enlarged, and would have to wait patiently as the image of the woman, from head to toe, would appear. Owing to the time it took for the picture to load on slow cable internet, the viewing of the static image became a virtual striptease: the blank, white screen would gradually disclose shapes and colours in horizontal bars that together resembled a woman's naked body. The young man would later learn in a graduate seminar that this unveiling or disclosure was much like a *blason*, in which a Renaissance poet might describe in metaphor and simile the features of a beautiful woman according to the sequence the young man had viewed a *Playboy* centrefold.

The young man had to admit that he treated these women, or rather images of women, as objects for his own use; as soon as he had relieved his urges, he forgot about them and did not even dream about them. In his conversations with other churchgoers of his age, he made no mention of his fantasy-processes. When he prayed aloud in a group, he occasionally confessed the sin of lust, which everyone knew men of his age suffered from (with the exception of a small number of engineers). He would have preferred to confess the sin of pride or anger or greed, but during certain trying weeks he could not deny serious lapses in purity and was compelled to confess them, despite the shame it inevitably entailed.

On a late Sunday morning at a park on a busy street in Milsons Point, a group of youth-group leaders sat in a circle to 'share and pray'. Among those leaders who were seated on the thick grass of the park was the young man, whose turn it was to disclose something of his spiritual life. Although the young man was embarrassed to say so, he confessed aloud that he had had one of those weeks in which lust had taken a firm grip of him, and there was no point in hiding it from his group of fellow youth leaders. After he had confessed the week's sins aloud in prayer, one after another youth leader confessed the sin that had been burdening him or her for some time. For many of the men the sin that oppressed them was also lust, but not always; the women spoke of neglect or callousness, of wronging a friend or a parent, or an outburst of anger that had destroyed a relationship. When they had finished this outpouring of confession, one by one they opened their eyes and felt unexpectedly relieved. Rather than censure the young man for revealing his serious lapses that week, they were grateful for his admission of weakness, for it gave them licence to unburden themselves of what they had been too afraid to acknowledge, let alone confess aloud; it made them remember that despite being youth leaders, they – like the youth they led and the ordinary churchgoers they mingled with – were also fallen creatures in need of grace.

The young man had to admit that in any other circumstance he would not have befriended any of the persons who were part of this group of youth leaders. He had barely thought of himself as a leader of the youth or of any age group, having been thrust from one position to another. He had almost nothing in common with the others in terms of personal tastes or interests, having grown up in a similar milieu yet having avoided, as much as possible, what was denoted by the term *popular culture*. He was largely unaware of the references or allusions they made to popular Hollywood movies or popular American television shows, nor was he able to identify, never mind sing, any number of the 'Top 40' songs that played repeatedly on commercial radio stations. Although he had a similar upbringing to them as an Australian-Born Chinese (or ABC, to use the common abbreviation) and assumed the adopted country of his Southeast Asian parents as his natural habitat, it was as if he were a recalcitrant who had forgotten or refused to cede his private world to the public, popular realm of things. Whenever a reference or allusion was made to a thing of this realm, he was a little embarrassed that he did not know what thing was referred or alluded to, but the young man made no effort to learn of the thing, choosing instead to spend his time studying, playing tennis, or listening to jazz recordings.

While the young man was a youth leader, he also attended literature and philosophy classes for several days a week at the University of New South Wales. Almost none of the other students who attended these classes were youth group leaders, nor did the young man see them around at the Christian group on campus which hosted hour-long talks on Tuesday and Thursday in the large auditorium at the top of the hill. During these talks, a beleaguered Anglican chaplain who wore old metal-rimmed glasses would sometimes explain and dismiss various theories of history with diagrams drawn on a transparent slide on an overhead projector, contrasting for instance the dialectical materialism of Marx (<) to the linear progression of Jesus' kingdom (—).There were other words projected on the diagrams, but the young man does not recall any of them; he only remembers that he was at a Christian conference primarily intended for undergraduates and the theme for the conference was *eschatology*. Despite five days of prayer meetings, Bible studies, seminars, and talks that were arranged on or around this theme, the young man would not be able to say afterwards what *eschatology* meant; but when the word was mentioned, he thought of the diagrams along with the word *tension*. Sometimes he saw a clock ticking at the eleventh hour, because a leader of one of his groups, who was known as a ministry training apprentice, had brought up the image while explaining the term. But most of the time the young man associated the theological term with the word *tension*, which he understood more precisely as a tension between what had happened when Jesus came, died, and rose from the dead, and his returning again to judge at the so-called second coming. This tension was encapsulated in the phrase *now but not yet*, a phrase the young man heard a great deal at the conference that was shorthand for the discrepancy that the kingdom was here but not completely, that Jesus had fulfilled the law and the prophets but had reserved some measure of fulfilment for his second visitation. The kingdom of God had already come, but in Sydney only a select group of Christians were aware of it.

For the four years that the young man was an undergraduate and a youth group leader, he attended the talks of this campus group each week during the semester as well as the mid-year conference during the winter semester break at a large rural property that went by the name *Merroo*. At the time the young

44

man called himself a Christian even though he did not know whether he was a Christian. Many of the things he did passed for being a Christian: he went to church every week, taught Sunday school, read the Bible and prayed, attended Christian talks and conferences and Bible studies, even was part of a ten-day mission in Gerroa, a holiday spot south of Sydney, where he and a Christian friend would walk from caravan to caravan to strike up a conversation to share the Good News or befriend teenage children who, because of a spinal deformity or some other aberration, were usually treated as outcasts. One of his mentors at the university, a ministry apprentice who had finished a bachelor's degree in chemistry, had asked him if he believed, and the young man had said that sometimes he wasn't sure if he was a Christian, but if someone were to ask him, point-blank, whether he was a Christian, he would immediately say that he was. Maybe that was proof enough that he was a Christian, the young man had said, and his mentor seemed to agree.

Throughout his childhood, the young man would often pray a prayer of confession that was expressly written for non-Christians wishing to convert. Although the evangelistic speaker said that those who were already Christians could substitute the words of the prayer to fit their circumstances, the teenager always prayed the prayer as if for the first time. Why so? Because no matter how often the teenager hunched over his Bible in confession or repented while trying to sleep, he could not shake the feeling that all was not forgiven – or that if all was, in the very near future there would be more to forgive.

Sometime between finishing high school and the second year of university, the young man stopped praying the prayer for himself. The young man committed many of the same sins as he

45

had as a teenager, but it seemed strange to pray the prayer as a youth leader. (Occasionally as a youth leader he gave evangelistic talks to teenagers and prayed the prayer aloud so they could whisper it in their hearts for the first time. In these instances, the young man did not so much pray the prayer as *say* the prayer for the sake of others.) He knew that since he was now a youth leader it would be inappropriate to pray the prayer, even privately. As serious as his sins were, he would have to be content with asking for ordinary forgiveness rather than being afforded the joys of committing his life (again) as a newly born Christian.

At this point in the narrative, the grown man could report that the young man who was a youth-group leader continued to give lessons, Sunday by Sunday, on certain passages of Scripture or a 'relevant' topic to the youth, as well as devise one or another skit that illustrated some point or message to be expounded in a Bible study or talk. Many of these skits, to use the term then, would draw on television shows that the young man hardly watched, but because his role was to minister to the youth, he found himself writing and performing scripts which aped the format of *Australian Idol* or another recent television import. Although he could not quote readily from *The Simpsons* or even dodge a footy tackle with ease, he could make use of his oratory skills, acquired at an early age, to captivate the youth. Whether it was true or not that he dressed, as his mother put it, like an old man, preferring his ribbed navy polo to a T-shirt emblazoned with FCUK, hardly anyone could deny his ability to act and, above all, speak. For when he mounted the pulpit to preach to the youths for the first time, many felt that he spoke with what the older leaders referred to as power.

In the years 2002 and 2003, the young man was asked to

give more and more Bible talks at the monthly youth service on Sunday mornings. He was also asked to host twenty-first birthday parties and youth-group camps, where the adult participants of both kinds of gatherings were much the same. In the third or fourth year as an undergraduate in an arts and social sciences faculty, years which correspond to the ones just cited, the young man was asked to give a talk at a so-called evangelistic event for teenagers on a Saturday night in the medium-sized hall behind the main church building. Several hours before the talk, the young man was hitting a tennis ball on the side wall of his parents' garage. The young man had not completed the talk, and thought by distracting himself with this game of mini-tennis that he would hit upon a good conclusion. The real difficulty, as he understood it, lay in coming up with a phrase that would encapsulate what had gone before and would serve, as it were, as a bridge to the concluding moment of the talk – leading, naturally, to a public prayer of conversion. The young man had learnt that such a phrase, as in Hollywood movies, ought to be mentioned throughout the talk in various contexts according to a certain beat, until the cumulative force of its repetition would result in a climactic revelation of sorts. And then the phrase, much like a magical talisman, would acquire a certain resonance in the listeners, and many of them would feel compelled, almost against their wills, to repeat in their hearts, as they were encouraged to do, the words of a prayer that was projected onto a white fabric screen.

As he continued to hit the ball against the wall or retrieve the ball from the backyard lawn or among the thin branches of the surrounding bushes, the young man began to realise that no resonant phrase would be forthcoming. Eventually the young man wrote something down, but when he looked at the words while he was preaching that night, he began to be aware of himself *reading* the script he had prepared. If up to this moment of the talk he had been *preaching* with the aid of a script, one could say that after this moment he had stopped preaching and begun simply *reading*. When the young man had paused near the end of the talk to look at the faces of one or several youths, he became aware of himself – that *he* was preaching to these youths – and when he returned his eyes to the part of the script he had written after hitting a tennis ball against a garage wall, he had lost most of his conviction.

After the talk one of the older youth-group leaders came up to the young man and thanked him for speaking, but the gratitude, if it could be called that, seemed forced. It was as if everyone had felt, but was perhaps unable to admit, that something apart from preaching had occurred. In one of the cards that all the youth filled out after the talk and the prayer, the young man read that some of the talk had come across as insincere and hollow. The youth who had written the comment was, as far as he knew, a Christian girl in her mid to late teens. When this comment was mentioned in the presence of several of his fellow leaders, most of them laughed it off; however insincere the delivery of the talk and the praying of the prayer, a few of the youths had nevertheless prayed the prayer for the first time. God was to be praised.

JARAD BRUINSTROOP
FIVE POEMS

Jarad Bruinstroop is a writer, PhD candidate and sessional academic at Queensland University of Technology. His work has appeared in *Meanjin*, *Overland*, *Island* (online), *Westerly*, *Australian Poetry Journal* and elsewhere. He was runner-up for the 2021 Thomas Shapcott Poetry Prize. He is the 2022 University of Queensland Fryer Library Creative Writing Fellow.

Two Cities

I.
Nobody in Rome cares
that I have begun
to devour you.
In the hostel this morning
and again tonight.
Even on the basilica stairs
while the nuns pray inside.

II.
Late fall is the time to begin
composing winter music—
when everything yearns
to be soft and lean.
At night the air
on the corner of Madison
and Fifty-seventh is faint
with hunger for snow.

Chartres Cathedral

The acolyte calls us each *monster*
when, for two francs, he unlocks the side gate.
Monsieur, you assure me
as we whisper through the dim interior.
Between the columns,
kaleidoscope windows flare in midday sun.
The glass here, they say,
is a blue found nowhere else.
Somewhere between deep Aegean
and Mary's robe.
Back in late autumn light
we stroll medieval streets
until, in a small churchyard,
we are swallowed by a wedding party.
A man in a cap eddies with his fiddle.
The guests call out two unmarried sisters.
We dance and watch each other.
It's impurities that make the blue unique—
a salting of ash in the kiln.

Scene from Bruges

From the bell tower, the city is an aquatint.
Rusted-hull roofs dry-docked for centuries
along the drab canals. Church steeple
pale as winter reed. Above us,
two peregrines nest behind the parapet.
Between the quarter-hour bells
their talons scrape the stone.
You could have written us like that.
Scraping out a life in this city.
Or any other. Far below us,
in the square, a woman is selling
the last Madonna lilies of summer.

Our Lady's Juggler

after Glyn Philpot's *Le Jongleur de Notre Dame* 1928

The cathedral made room for a juggler
because he was handsome in the light
of heaven. In front of the statue of Mary,
Mother of God, he threw everything
up into the air – grace, faith, and his own
lithe physique. Like Jesus, he performed
tricks with his body. Like Jesus, his sweat fell
to the ground like great drops of blood.
Not actual blood. A simile. Still,
he waited for the statue to embrace him.

Caravaggisti

after Giovanni Baglione

You painted the three men twice
in almost the same configuration.
First, the angel wears plate armour
and the devil's head is turned away.
Later, the angel is dressed in silk
and the devil wears your enemy's face.
Cupid remains naked in both paintings.
Explain to me again, my love,
the difference between jealousy
and envy. I remember
it has something to do
with a desire to possess.

ANIELA RODRIGUEZ
CAIN'S FEAST

...for a bullet had taken him that far, to the Sixth Circle, where
he had confirmed that hell is just as we imagine.

Ignacio Padilla

Translated by Elizabeth Bryer

Aniela Rodríguez was born in Chihuahua in 1992 and has a master's degree in modern letters from the Universidad Iberoamericana. She won the 2013 Chihuahua Prize for Literature with *El confeccionador de deseos*, and the Comala National Young Short Story Prize 2016 with *El problema de los tres cuerpos*. She has also published the poetry collection *Insurgencia*.

Elizabeth Bryer is the author of *From Here On, Monsters*, which was joint winner of the 2020 Norma K. Hemming Award. She is also a translator from Spanish, including of novels by María José Ferrada, Aleksandra Lun, José Luis de Juan and Claudia Salazar Jiménez. She lives on unceded sovereign Wurundjeri land.

In memoriam
To my beloved Nacho, since this feast
is more yours than mine

THE SHOT JACINTO DELIVERED HIM that day was enough for the priest to realise that heaven is a shitty invention: the futile drivel of the missals and leaflets matrons dispense when proclaiming the blessedness of Our Lord. First light was enough for us to find ourselves leaving church singing hallelujahs and giving thanks to God, for the sky to blacken and the organ to be struck dumb due to some fault in its moving parts or an anomaly in the hearts of men.

Jacinto went rigid at the door. He wasn't going to try anything, by God he didn't want to shoot him. He had backed out of it to start with. To forget, he stepped inside the cantina, where he tossed back the bottle of whisky that was set down in front of him; it didn't obliterate his shame, but it did give him the courage to grab the pistol his mother kept in the chest of drawers, second from the top behind the photograph of his dead father and the little socks from when he was a newborn. He was such a beautiful infant, people said, he would smile every time he was blessed, how could we have expected such a thing from the boy Jacinto when he was so good. May God be with that poor child and may He have mercy on his soul.

The day Jacinto found out Francisca was pregnant, the sky closed over and the rain pelted down in a way nobody had seen around those parts for years. The clouds blackened and the gale's howling turned into a bald-faced silence, for the girl had been carrying the fruit of her wrongdoing in her belly for three whole months and not a soul had noticed. At the end of the day, he had done all he could to set her on a new path. They had known each other since they were kids, but when she was fifteen she had gone to the capital in search of work to support her family. And for what: it was enough to stumble across a pimp who sent her to work in La Doblado and pocketed a third of her takings. When Francisca started to get a name for herself, the son of a bitch asked for half her earnings; that was when things blew up and she came home.

Nobody goes back to the place they were born with their luck all bent out of shape, but there she was: fucked over, her hair unkempt, looking to patch up her life through any new turn of events. So every now and then she slipped on her Sunday outfit and the heels one of her clients had given her and went to the main square to salvage her lost youth, though nobody approached her out of disgust, though everyone thought she stank and God had reserved a special place for her in the furnaces of hell, a woman tossed in the trash, may the peace of the Lord have mercy on your ailing soul.

How to believe in a God who brings suffering into the world and grants us peace without considering our sorrows, thought Jacinto, tottering like a small child. In one hand he held a half-empty bottle of rum and in the other the revolver he took from his mother. More than thirteen years had passed since his father died; in all that time he had never felt as alone as today, when Francisca confessed to him on her knees that the child wasn't his and she was carrying a monster in her belly. The woman knelt, and, gazing at her from above, the man went over every word ever invented to describe what he felt in his chest. Jacinto stopped listening; he was thinking of his father's face the day he said the word cancer and sat down in the cane chair to await death. It arrived three months later with no cry of pain: he simply rolled over in bed and noticed the slug of phlegm in his throat that was getting harder to swallow, that was making his skin stiffer and stiffer, till the minute he stopped feeling anything and hung his head like a chicken about to die.

How to believe in a God who watches on as the priest strokes your woman's leg and croons in her ear the beatitudes of Christ. May God forgive all your sins and drag you by one foot to hell and may you be greeted by legions of demons screaming your name and pawing the cauldron where your flesh might be scorched, your eyes might fill with tears and your perversions might be noted. For fuck's sake, Francisca, fuck all the whores in the world who fake tears and stand around with their hands in their pockets. Fuck the hopes of old and ailing men who die deprived of the consolation of a woman in their bed, may God forgive you today and forever, may He wash your wounds and bless you with a healthy child.

Since the day she arrived back in town, Francisca hadn't slept without seeing beasts with enormous maws. She hid her longing to fall apart, but nobody could relieve her of the weight of all the women she had been those nights in the capital. Without giving it much thought, she awaited her turn in the confessionary of the town cathedral. She went in without the slightest care and, standing before the priest, let drop a string of heresies that would make anybody's hair stand on end.

The priest nodded at all Francisca's secrets and for penance gave her fifty Our Fathers and twenty-five Hail Marys to be intoned aloud in perfect solitude. From the depths of his being, he pardoned the woman who confessed to having slept with more than fifty men. He was obliged by his faith to console the faithful and so let his fingers, wettened with holy water, graze her forehead, and that was when he started imagining all the caresses that had begun with the simple brush of her fingertips. He dried the girl's tears and started to think about the way Francisca's lips parted to receive the communion of carnal love.

Only Jacinto knew of the infected sore of his marriage, a stain that would never be scrubbed away even with a change of clothes or towns. Believe in God above all else and fortune will rain down, said Jacinto, not moving. He kept drinking from the bottle while in the background the guitarrón strummed one of the many songs repeated from bar to bar. A man in the corner of the cantina racked his brain for the song lyrics; unable to remember, he swayed above the empty beer bottles and, like a fly stunned by a newspaper, fell unconscious to the table. I liked that you left in December, the other drunks kept singing, till the silence grew heavier and there was nothing to be heard but the thumps of the glasses on the bar. Nobody said a word now, they all stopped and listened to how Jacinto's tears thundered to the beat of the booze. María, the bartender, rubbed his head. She tucked the bill into his hand and sent him home with four bruisers who didn't have enough money to keep drinking themselves stupid. Amid the voices sounded the toasts and the songs that quickly spread the name of Jacinto, the picture of betrayal, who at the first opportunity got up and left the cantina to the patrons' chorus: I'm not starting the new year with a love who does me wrong.

He had to walk for almost an hour to get to the jacal built on the highest part of the ridge. Hot stones worked their way through the holes in his shoes. The man on whom Jacinto intended to offload his anger was wearing a straw sombrero about to fall to pieces. You would be don Pancho, wouldn't you? You got that right, the other replied, lifting the brim on the right side to squint at him. He looked at him as only tough guys do, withered by the glare of the sun and the plough. I don't get what you're doing here, why not take off to the city. Jacinto took a cigarette from his bag and sat on the kerb: what you don't get, don Pancho, is that it's like having a splinter buried in my chest. The other didn't bat an eyelid. He turned and blew smoke in his face. The sun announced midday and the lizards started emerging from their holes. The town was covered in a dense sheet of dust that stretched to the horizon. Now I really don't get you, kid. One day you come looking for your father and the next you're obsessing over a whore, what do you want me to do?

Show me how to shoot this fucker, Jacinto smiled, still holding the ash-filled stub between his fingers. Straight away don Pancho recognised the boy's locked jaw, same as his father's so many years ago. He asked no more questions. He took the revolver from the table and let a bullet escape into the dust cloud. It slipped through and was lost like a coral snake between the huisaches.

There was nowhere to hide. The bullet drew an unsteady line, like Jacinto's gait. The organ kept playing a good while, till an out-of-tune note brought it to a halt. The screams of the choir rang out, as did those of the lectors and the altar boys who, still clutching the thurible, ran to help the fallen man. Jacinto remembered his wife's confession as if he had lived it too. Between saints and hallelujahs, the priest had put his hand on her leg, just like that, uninvited. Despite her reluctance, he took her in silence to the priory, where he spoke very softly about the unmentionable. They didn't come back out after that; poor Francisca was spreadeagled on the floor like a cat, enduring the holy onslaught of the priest. Fucking hell, Francisca, if only you had been a cat and not Jacinto's woman.

He wasn't going to try anything, by God he didn't want to shoot him. He would be a fool to want to kill a priest, but nobody knows what is to come: I started out as a goddamn carpenter's assistant, I got five hundred pesos a week, barely enough for essentials. I told you, Francisca, stop despairing, someday you would find a job that would get us out of poverty and mean we could go back to the city, build ourselves a little house, forget the sidelong glances and the gossipy old women. I wanted to come home from work with a little box hidden in my jacket, get down on my knee and tell you the words you always wanted to hear, my Francisca, wanted to give you a ring as big and beautiful as the hills rising in the distance that we look at every afternoon when the sun's rays get all tousled by those hills' curves.

Francisca turned around. Only Jacinto remembers the moment she stopped time to tell him she would follow the ways of the Lord, hitched up the ruffles of her skirt and tried to apologise for her neglect. She kept track of the men she had slept with and was sure that once again, just like on other occasions, she had fucked everything up. She also knew she was still very young and, if she wanted, she could ruin her life another seven times over. She didn't say anything else to Jacinto. She wasn't in love. She

64

was going to have the baby because for some time now she had been tempting fate and getting away with it. Jacinto had started crying, cursing each of his ancestors for giving him the dog luck of getting tangled up with a backcountry whore.

Francisca turned around. She was careful about the sound her steps were making on the sidewalk. She remembered the furrowed brow of the priest when he told her that hell doesn't have room for all that many souls. And if you're careful, he murmured in her ear, you can have the best of both worlds, and Francisca took his hand, trying to understand the meaning of his words, and Francisca shut her eyes, pretending not to feel the cassock slide across her thighs, and Francisca squatted down.

Only Jacinto remembers the thundering of his tears when they fell to the floor, when, swollen with rage, he stopped crying to take off his trousers and stare at the portrait of his father, who observed him from where he was nestled in one of the drawers between old underwire bras and shameless love letters. It was the only gravestone Jacinto had known, the only place where he could pay his respects to the private who smiled in a yellowing photograph, shouting, deep inside, the only word he had uttered since the day he closed the door and rolled over in bed.

The charging bullet was enough to remind the priest what colour the devil's eyes are. He was slow to recognise the crackle of gunpower in his guts. At first it was a coldness, like what you feel when you're about to fall asleep and a jerk yanks you back into the world. Then, the wound began to grow so large that he noted very clearly how his limbs shrank. He looked at Jacinto, whose shirt was untucked and whose belt was dancing in its loops. Little was left of the smile that made Francisca quiver on the floor of that narrow room and turned her into a cat on heat. The bullet penetrated his belly: at first it seemed cold and then like the hot horn of a bull. A fever started rising in him and as it did he wished he had never shown up to deliver the sermon that day.

The priest was overcome by thirst and in a few seconds his muscles grew heavy. In his head he recognised Francisca's name. He had no time to regret anything; he looked at Jacinto's left hand still holding the revolver. Jacinto paused a moment, with the need for who knows what. The priest remembered Jacinto as a boy running in the atrium, rolling around in glee beneath the altar while up there the crucified figure of Christ was trembling in anguish from the three nails. He squeezed the rosary and had no option but to listen to the last notes of the organ, while the choir of old ladies repeated in unison: Blessed is every one that feareth the Lord; that walketh in his ways!

KATE CROWCROFT
TONGUE BROKEN

Kate Crowcroft is a writer and artist. She received her doctorate on the medical history of the mouth and tongue from the University of Cambridge. In 2020 she was a Copyright Agency Creative Writing Fellow. Her debut book *Tongue* is forthcoming.

MY RESEARCH ON THE TONGUE was divided across the equator, the exhaust offset. In the northern winter I hurtled south towards the summer, to Split Point | Wathaurong land. *The cabin lights will be dimmed for landing.* 'Research' comes from Old French *recercher* which means 'to search closely', from *cercher* 'to seek for', through Latin *circare*, 'to wander, traverse', from *circus*, for circle. Returning to that divided kingdom a few weeks later, London glinting below as bared teeth, over the speaker would come the refrain: *this is customary when flying in the hours of darkness.*

The roads were icy that February morning and the sky overcast, and the temperature scarcely rose inside the library. I was following a lead on a pamphlet popular in nineteenth-century New York called *The Tongue of Time.* It covered the natural and spiritual worlds, disease, witchcraft, trances, dreams, death, diet, serpents, opium use, the childbearing of older women, mouth care and hygiene, accounts of people with two souls, and the universality of deception.

With each flight the stairs narrowed, spiralling inward until I stepped out into clouds of my own breath. Through the slat on the landing a hard sunless light, livid in colour, was moving along the floor, over drifts of books known as the overflow. The landing felt as though it were shifting ever so slightly from side to side, doubtless a psychological effect of the spiralling staircase and the narrowness. And I had been told that, so close to the tower, the sound of the wind alone could produce that effect, the effect of an edge, vertigo, as standing on the end of a pier. It felt familiar, the volatility that pervaded everything I read about the organ. What was the human tongue? The last animal of the face's reserve. Through the slat I saw a sail of white birds lift and fall up and beyond the brickwork.

I had until that morning been looking for stories of women, saints or otherwise, whose tongues had been cut out at the root. In many of these tales, speaking again after the violence is the point of the story (it's a miracle) but I was redirected when I came across *The Tongue of Time*. The archive boxes were arranged in dim rows extending from a main corridor, strings of dormant cells. The light there was controlled by a timer, itself a bone-neon more commonly found in hospitals and apartment complex stairwells. I turned the dial and the minutes began to run down.

Some of the boxes had ink markings from previous systems, disintegrated letters and numbers the colour of sandstone. I found *The Tongue of Time* and sat on the floor with the overflow to read it. When I finished I made a brief note for reference, in case I needed to revisit the work in a year or two: *Stories, mainly allegorical, myths, moral directives. The tongue is employed as a metaphor for the extension and consumption of aeons, the way time laps at one's heels. It contains conflicted and disparate worlds, confessions, issues and arguments of all kinds*. I placed the pamphlet carefully back in the box and returned it to its cell.

My relationship with the tongue began with an incision made on my father's body. He was leaning on the drip looking bad enough to be redeemed. The hot purple wound ran from his solar plexus to the base of his gut – in medical terms, an incision from the xiphoid process to the pubic symphysis. To the eyes of a child he had been opened along his length and stapled back together. And I felt it then, soundless, the stuck muscle in my mouth become stone. This was a long time ago.

Towards the end of his life my father would sit in the garden and I brought him things he could eat. The last thing he could eat was soft bread. 'Break it into pieces,' he said, and I did as instructed. What voice would I have needed (were there words I could have used?) that might have opened a final kindness between he and I. But here are his arms in sheets of skin outstretched for the bread, our faces set. And the vapour of my voice held for so long it alchemised into feeling: *the relief of his becoming weaker.*

Break it into pieces. They were the last words he said to me. The word 'archive' comes from *arkhē* (ἀρχή) Ancient Greek for 'beginning place' or 'point of origin'. Meanings evolved to 'written records' and the public buildings in which they are kept. Archives are patient, dependent on care and active listening for creation and survival. To assemble an archive is to piece things together. But its parts gesture to how much we cannot know, to how much is missing and may not be recovered. Go far down into the word ἀρχή and you find water. The root comes out at the ocean, or rather the cosmic ocean – a yawning elemental chaos from which all supposedly emerged.

In the library café, on my break, I read in a magazine that our oldest and most primitive vertebrate ancestor *Saccorhytus coronarius* was a big mouth with no anus. Fossils from around five hundred and forty million years ago reveal its mouth-body was no bigger than a grain of black rice. This first creature was covered with a thin skin and lived in the sands of the seabed. It is unlikely that *Saccorhytus coronarius* is a direct human ancestor, but the creature tells us about the early stages of our evolution – it had bilateral symmetry, two symmetrical halves.

Of women's mutilated tongues, I had a particular interest in stories where the breakage was self-inflicted. Self-muted and deeply bitten, sacrificed in order to save something else. In effect, self-censored to prevent what could come to light. Like the story of Tymicha for example, in the Syrian philosopher Iamblichus's *Life of Pythagoras* which dates to the sixth century BCE. Persecuted under the tyrant Dionysius, she bites off her tongue when threatened with torture. Tymicha then repurposes the organ as a physical weapon and spits it at him in defiance. The story makes it clear that, being female and prone to talkativeness, she breaks her tongue because she might not be able to govern it, and may instead be *compelled to disclose something that ought to be concealed in silence.*

For years, being quiet, I felt clear. Clear and cool. I tended the lies of others – I packaged them like cold cuts and offered safe keeping, or gave them safe passage onward to fortify other stories. And this was care-work, a craft even, with its own bruised grace inside a culture that could not be changed, a familial system that needed to be preserved for a kind of survival.

Later, I gathered pieces of information about the tongue. The rare books and documents smelt delicious, like old-growth forest – a rich earthiness rose from their pages. Others of vellum were salty in scent, soft to the touch and made no sound, the membrane silent when turned over. I thumbed metaphorical bodies: *The Anatomy of the Soul, The Anatomy of Melancholy, The Anatomy of a Woman's Tongue, The Anatomy of Abuses.* I ran the tip of my index finger along the spines, letting the timer that controlled the light run down, shut off, working in half-light. No longer minding, no longer noticing.

The treatment of the tongue revealed cultures of violence and fear, and the organ required special thought and care in its use. But in the negotiation of this contested site, writings on the tongue also demonstrated, by virtue of their moralising, how closely care and control could be interwoven.

The following spring I presented an extract at a seminar to share some initial findings on the historical treatment of the tongue.

Extract.
The organ itself is longitudinally separated into symmetrical right and left sides by a section of fibrous tissue, the lingual septum, that results in a groove or furrow on the tongue's surface called the median sulcus. This is the line that scores the tongue through the middle. The philosophy of anatomy housed an assumption that the truth of a moral blueprint within could be excised – an old logic that married physiological markers with divine design. Moral topographies were written in sinew and bone. The view inside the tongue at its dividing line provided a glimpse of what stuff lay under the inscription at the surface. For moralists, the line evoked the anatomical duality of the flesh, and recalled an inherently deceitful organ. The tongue was mapped morally long before the organ was laid out on the slab, and it has been read and written over long after. My interests lie here, in the dissection. The sixteenth-century Belgian anatomist Andreas Vesalius made an incision down the median sulcus, butterflying the tongue, opening it out. The dissection revealed its shape when cut from the body, giving it a physical presence beyond its relationships with the palate, teeth, lips, and larynx or voice box. The tongue's dual

physiological landscape was examined where it cleaves, displayed according to the fissure.

Tongue | Language || Lingua

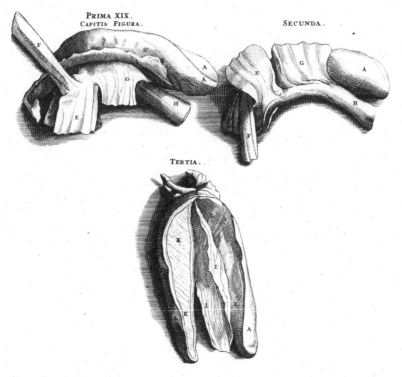

Plates from Andreas Vesalius' *On the Fabric of the Human Body,* 1543.

After the seminar a man who had made a comment disguised as a question approached me at the wine table. He was a historian by trade and had I read Latour? (I had not.) 'Thank you for your question,' I said. We chatted for some time until I noticed the room had thinned out. He leant toward me and confided that he hears voices in the archive, the voices of the dead asking to be heard. Did I hear them too? 'No,' I said. 'I don't hear voices exactly.' 'What then?' he asked. 'It's more like the presence of things I can't remember,' I said. Words rarely came to my aid like that and although what I'd said made little logical sense, he nodded as though it made sense to him. He was looking down, eyes on his empty glass. I asked him if he felt they were actual voices, the voices he heard. He nodded again and put his glass with the others. 'Tell anyone and I'll kill you,' he said. It was very important to him, he explained, that his work in the academy was serious work. He was known in particular among his colleagues for the scientific rigour he brought to his field of historiography. I touched my left collar bone at the indent and found the strap of my bag slung there. I said I had to go. SALIVA! he cried suddenly, with an intensity that seemed both haphazard and precise. And he bubbled something about how spittle is a portal to the past. 'All your ancestors back to the Neanderthals are contained inside your saliva!' he said, the room now empty but for the two of us.

The tongue had been made to wear its apparent proclivity for slipperiness and deceit (readings were made into its ecosystem and appearance). It was simply the best instrument we had for our projections. Interesting to consider, too, that words often have their genesis in the material. 'Mendacity' comes from the Latin word *mendax* (lie) and has the root stem -*mend*, meaning 'physical defect, fault'. This is also the source of the Sanskrit word *minda*, 'physical blemish', and the Old Irish *mennar*, 'stain'. The lie carries these residues: a mark, a taint, the fleshly defect as sign. On another branch, the root stem -*mend* leads to 'amend' – to free from faults, to set right, to make better.

Among the rows of boxes, with one bar of reception, my mother and I sent each other messages. I asked her about her day; I asked her questions about the past. She was often forthcoming, but equally often I felt like I was tipping a Magic Eight Ball upside down, shaking it, asking it to prophesy a pathway back instead of forward. I waited for her reply as though watching the triangle emerge from the watery murk with its abrupt, perplexing message.

Why did you make me lie about the violence?
No answer. It was not the right question. I tried a different one.
What, in your view, did my father lie about?
She came online. She was typing...
Everything.
And then she disappeared again, to *last seen*.

Different kinds of silence have their own idioms; they are passed down in family cultures. The wound on my father's body concealed a tumour the size and shape of a fist. Deep in his abdomen it sprouted and metastasised until the evidence of its presence broke the surface, necessitating the line that divided his body into a right side and a left. That a text can be read allegorically does not make it an allegory. Allegory, by definition, contains instructions for its own interpretation. I read my father's body as confession. I traced words to their roots, I traced words for lying, for different kinds of lie in different languages. I believed if I went back far enough I could find understanding, or rather an answer would be there, waiting for me. Leaving the library after dark, walking past the rows towards the stairs at the end of the corridor, I saw my father, stapled crudely along his length, the drip drip drip of the saline solution, the riddle of him trying to work itself out of itself.

Before this, during my first year of research, I became concerned that my interest in the tongue was devolving into obsession, even addiction, and I told Theo I would not be continuing. She just frowned and said nothing. The next time I saw her she pressed a copy of Augustine's *Confessions* into my hand. 'Who takes care of the past?' she said. Her words felt like a contract signed under duress. I laughed (fear; grief?). Until that point I hadn't considered the past to be something that needed looking after.

In his essay *A Plague of Mendacity*, the Egyptian-American cultural critic Ihab Hassan wrote that lying may be a riddle deeper than language itself. It is wise to remember that the most adroit methods of innate deception have evolved for survival. Animal pretends to be plant, plant pretends to be animal. Mimicries of shape, colour and scent saw some flowers outlive dinosaurs. In the temperate waters where I was raised, a crab decorates its carapace with algae and seaweeds to move undetected by predators. In the desert, a tongue orchid tricks a wasp into sex.

I met Theodora in a line waiting to hear Judith Butler speak on the topic of vulnerability. I held my place in the queue for an hour or so when it began to rain and my eyes fell on her back, on her sweater soaking up each droplet, until I could make out the spectres of two shoulder blades. She glanced back at me and smiled. I looked up and let the rain fall over my face. People ahead were being turned away at the door; the hall had filled to capacity. When this news filtered along the line a man behind me broke down at volume. I have thought often of him since, of his loud crying and how no one said a thing to him, how everybody left him there like he carried a taint, as though we might catch the thing that makes one reveal too much.

Etymologically, the lie contains residues of fault, but it is also the case that a truth can feel tainted, necessitating a lie. The truth of his need – of our need – felt marked, raw and vulgar the moment he stopped pretending he was fine. Saturated, I walked back to my attic room and thought about the Janus face of this problem, the messy truths we lie for, and the ways that those lies afford us a gritty shroud in less-than-ideal systems.

When I got home, I dried off and watched a YouTube clip of Butler talking about queer alliances. A queer alliance, they told a happily seated audience, is unpredictable and improvised, and might be a response to crisis. It is also, they said, a response to historical necessity. I would go back, see if he was okay – he might be gone, I thought – when there was the woman in the white sweater on the other side of my door. 'I'm Theo,' she said. She was out of breath, and wet. She had followed me back and let herself in to the building.

I lived those college years in an attic with rising damp, listening to creatures moving in the walls, eating them out. The foundations of that place were rotted to the core. After Theo left I prepared coffee for a night of work ahead, and I read about protocols and devices used to enforce breakage. The bit and bridle had its inception in the British Isles in the Middle Ages. Records show it was principally used on those accused of gossiping, women who were thought to be outspoken or vying for power, or wives who moved beyond the boundaries of what their husbands and communities deemed suitable for them. The bridle held the head and face in iron and a two-inch rod was inserted into the mouth, clamping and flattening the tongue to prevent movement.

Learning by mouth was visceral. The bit and bridle would reshape the tongue, a technology that saw a violence upon the mouth-site designed to bring it into line and change the organ's muscle memory. The device was repurposed for the long project of colonisation, used to break the will of people taken to the Americas from their African homelands. What began with preventing speech was used as an index for the entire body. By going inside the mouth, body and mind could be silenced and reordered, reorienting a person towards another's will.

I thought about what tongues are used for and what they can do, from the tip to the root. There is a habit of weakened use, a soft inheritance – a muscle trained in how not to move, how not to work. This habit may be rehearsed to non-use; *rehearsed.* The French naturalist Lamarck's first law: more frequent and continuous use of any organ gradually strengthens, develops and enlarges that organ, and gives it a power proportional to the length of time it has been so used; while the permanent disuse of any organ imperceptibly weakens and deteriorates it, and progressively diminishes its functional capacity, until it finally disappears.

So, if a speaker stops using their tongue (not knowing why, or having chosen to stop using it, or having been violently forced to do so) over time eventually it seems like it was never meant to be used in that way. The idea here, the misbelief so pernicious and arresting, is that your tongue was never yours to use.

Theo helped me to remain present, remain focussed on what mattered. One night as we lay in bed she turned to me and smiled and touched her thumb to my cheek bone, my temple. 'In the country where I grew up, we could be jailed for what we just did,' she said.

There are many ways to break a tongue, and there are many ways to recall its power, not only as an instrument of speech that shapes sound within its home of the mouth and palate, but as an organ involved in knowledge acquisition, sense making, flights and figment. In one fifteenth-century record from Europe, under the right moral and structural conditions, the tongue itself was believed to be a portal to hidden knowledge. The moon had to be in the right position, and the tongue and mouth needed to be washed clean, then certain precious stones placed under the tongue at the tie would allow visions of the future to be revealed. Ordinary people carried out the ritual. The organ was a threshold, a line or pathway bridging temporal and spiritual mysteries.

What did those everyday folk feel or hear or see, I wondered? With all the parts in their right places, the precious stone under the tongue, and the moon up there on full. Those people believed in the tongue as a piece of psychic apparatus, as an organ that could bring fortunes to light. I spent a lot of time thinking about those people. I wondered, when everything aligned, if they saw the very day and moment they were in: where the past had brought them and where their future was being made. When what one had known, and what one would come to know, opened inward to unfold the present, imparting oneself to oneself like an actual miracle.

In the life of Saint Christina, her pagan father has her flesh torn off with hooks, her legs broken. Christina throws her flesh pieces at him: *eat the flesh that you begot!* The story spirals downward in this vein. He has her rocked in an iron cradle of hot oil and resin like a newborn babe. She is then paraded through the city naked with her head shaved, but when thrown in a furnace with snakes for five days they only lick the sweat off her skin. At the end of all this her tongue is cut out and, never losing her voice, she throws the severed thing at her tormentor, blinding him in the eye. Tongue flesh as *pièce de resistance*.

I assembled some pieces as instructed, gathering evidence for a confession I could not make or that I'd forgotten how to make or amend, make amends, make good, make it good, rehearse, *rehearse* – from *rehersen*, to give an account, to report, to tell, to narrate a story; to speak or write words; repeat, reiterate; from Old French *rehercier*, to go over again, repeat, literally *to rake over*, turn over soil or ground, to drag (on the ground), to be dragged along the ground; to harrow the land; rip, tear, wound; repeat, rehearse, from *hearse*: a framework hung over the dead. From *herse*, a harrow, from *hirpus* for wolf, in reference to its teeth (Oscan language, extinct). An avowal I held down like a job.

The night after I read *The Tongue of Time*, I dreamt that the scar on my father's body was on my body. Waking to the taste of blood in my mouth, left incisor lodged on my tongue, a pain gradient revealed my jaw locked like a door. In the dream I am in the library trying to cram my organs back inside my body. I don't have any staples, so I'm attempting to close the skin of my torso like a winter coat. This approach is reasonably effective but the experience of having my guts spill into my hands has been embarrassing. I'm glad no one really visits this wing of the library. I hear the familiar turn of the timer and feel a thin light shiver through the gaps. When I reach the row and look at the dial it reads zero. I know that when I peer down there I will see a chair against the far wall with a box on it and although I want to pretend this is safe, if I walk down the row holding myself and reach the box I know the light will cut, in other words, a trap, and then I'm here.

Sources
Gordon Teskey, *Allegory and Violence*, Cornell University Press, 1996.
Jean-Baptiste Lamarck, *Zoological Philosophy*, Musée d'Histoire Naturelle, 1809.
Sara Ahmed, *What's the Use?*, Duke University Press, 2019.

My gratitude to Sean Borodale.

IMAN MERSAL
FIVE POEMS

Translated by Robyn Creswell

Iman Mersal is an Egyptian poet and Professor of Arabic Language and Literature at the University of Alberta. She is the author of five books of poetry and an essay collection, *How to Mend: Motherhood and Its Ghosts*. Her collection, *The Threshold* (trans. Robyn Creswell), will be published in late 2022.

Robyn Creswell teaches comparative literature at Yale and is the author of *City of Beginnings: Poetic Modernism in Beirut*.

The employee

She said to him, When a woman informs you that she's a little drunk
this is actually a warning that she's liable to collapse at any moment.
And when she tells you of a lost happiness
she means that you're responsible for giving it back to her
on a silver platter, like those knights in the stories of Caliphs
who return home with the heads of enemies on their spears.
She continued, And when she sits next to you in the office
just as I'm sitting next to you right now
you must listen to her while placing your right hand on top of her left.

The woman spoke in rather husky tones,
which wasn't appropriate with a man like that, so wide-eyed,
but as for me, I sat and calmly listened
to these passionate words of wisdom
delivered by an employee to her colleague at work.

A man decides to explain to me what love is

One day, a man decided to explain to me what love is. He was buttoning up his shirt while shadows gathered in the corners and the afternoon light crossed from one side of the room to the other. He seemed only half there, as when the screen dims and everyone in the movie theatre starts looking for exit signs. It was then, glasses tidily fixed around the backs of his ears, that he decided to explain to me what love is.

In the half-lit room he murmured, 'Love is actually a quest for...,' I opened my eyes and saw a band of conquistadors searching for gold in remotest Chile, hungry and dejected, while an Indian crouches behind a rock in fear. And when he said, 'Love is being truly content with...,' I began to hear the voice of Ella Fitzgerald and pressed my fingers into a mound of black chocolate. And when he said, 'It is a happiness which...,' well, I really couldn't imagine anything at all.

I'm sure I never saw that man again, because I never got to ask him if love is forgetting one's watch by the bedside.

Description of a migraine

I wanted to describe my chronic migraine
as one piece of evidence
that the chemical processes
occurring in my wonderful brain
were working effectively.

I intended to begin
My two hands aren't enough to prop my head up
but wrote instead:
A bullet from an unseen gun rips into
peaceful dimness
complete disorientation
fracture
a thousand separate splinters—
and also the pleasure
of arousing the sore spots
simply by remembering them.

A life

This didn't happen in my family home – no, not among those who know me (or so I once believed).

My life, the life I've never been able to touch, never been able to find a picture showing just the two of us – that life is next to me on my bed, opening her eyes after a long slumber and stretching her limbs, like a princess who knows that her father's palace is magically protected against thieves, and that although the wars never seem to end, happiness lies just beneath the skin.

This is the life into which more than one father stuffed his ambitions, more than one mother her scissors, more than one doctor his pills, more than one activist his sword, more than one institution its stupidity, and more than one school of poetry its poetics.

My life that I've lugged with me from city to city, running out of breath while chasing it from school to library, from the kitchen to the bar, from the flute to the piano, from Marx to the museums, from the memory of a body's smell to the dream of an airport lounge, from everything that I don't know to everything that I don't know. My life, whose existence I've never been sure of, lies next to me on my bed, opening her eyes after a long slumber and stretching her limbs, like a princess who knows that her father's palace is magically protected against thieves, and that although the wars never seem to end, happiness lies just beneath the skin.

This is how I awoke in that strange land the morning I turned forty, and if it weren't for the fact that God has never once chosen a woman, I'd have said it was the first sign of prophethood. If it weren't for my own peculiar way of thinking, I'd cite Mahmoud

Darwish about *a woman who entered her forties with perfect apricots*, or else the words of Miłosz: *I felt a door opening in me and I entered.*

I see before me a long line of the dead – dead, perhaps, because I loved them – and I see the homes designed for insomnia, which I always cleaned very carefully during the holidays, and the gifts I never opened, and the poems stolen from me line by line until I doubted whether they were ever mine, and men I only met at the wrong times, and clinics of which I remember nothing but the bars on their windows. I see my whole life before me and I could even embrace her if I wished, or sit on her lap and sing, or wail.

The book of desire

With his hand
by my hair
a man pulled me up
when I was drowning after walking
on water
an ark made of gold split in two
with a forest in the middle
and a sun that was like the sun
a cinereous wave of velvet but no ashes
a museum for everything extinct
and still deeper down
tiny fish swam into my lungs
and by my hair
with his hand
a man pulled me up until I twisted in the wind
time streamed past
and the mountains wavered between flames and light
all this happened and then I was back onshore
my dress torn
feeling the sand's firmness
and now that I'm here
I'm not frightened of the sea
for the closed book of desire
is open
with a bookmark on one of its pages.

New Titles from Giramondo

Fiction

Norman Erikson Pasaribu *Happy Stories, Mostly* (trans. Tiffany Tsao)

Jessica Au *Cold Enough for Snow*

Max Easton *The Magpie Wing*

Zarah Butcher-McGunnigle *Nostalgia Has Ruined My Life*

Pip Adam *Nothing to See*

Non-fiction

Bastian Fox Phelan *How to Be Between*

Antigone Kefala *Late Journals*

Evelyn Juers *The Dancer: A Biography for Philippa Cullen*

Gerald Murnane *Last Letter to a Reader*

Anwen Crawford *No Document*

Vanessa Berry *Gentle and Fierce*

Poetry

Lionel Fogarty *Harvest Lingo*

Tracy Ryan *Rose Interior*

Claire Potter *Acanthus*

Adam Aitken *Revenants*

J.S. Harry *New and Selected Poems*

Andy Jackson *Human Looking*

Eunice Andrada *Take Care*

Jane Gibian *Beneath the Tree Line*

For more information visit giramondopublishing.com/books/

Subscribe Now
And receive each issue of HEAT
Australia's international literary magazine

Since its inception in 1996, HEAT has been renowned for a dedication to
quality and a commitment to publishing innovative and imaginative poetry,
fiction, essays and hybrid forms. Now, in the third series, we are excited to
bring together a selection of the most interesting and adventurous Australian
and overseas writers. HEAT Series 3 is posted to subscribers every two months,
forming a unique, cohesive whole. Your subscription supports independent
literary publishing and enables us to cultivate and champion new and
challenging writing.

Visit giramondopublishing.com/heat/ to subscribe.

Submission Guidelines
HEAT welcomes submissions of fiction, essays, poetry and translated works
throughout the year. We encourage writing which gives full rein to the author's
voice, without the restriction of a word limit. In the case of poetry, we seek
longer poems, or a selection or sequence of poems. For further information,
please visit our website.

Acknowledgements

We respectfully acknowledge the Gadigal, Burramattagal and Cammeraygal peoples, the traditional owners of the lands where Giramondo's offices are located. We extend our respects to their ancestors and to all First Nations peoples and Elders.

HEAT Series 3 Number 3 has been prepared in collaboration with Ligare Book Printers, Avon Graphics, Ball & Doggett paper suppliers and Candida Stationery; we thank them for their support.

The Giramondo Publishing Company is grateful for the support of Western Sydney University in the implementation of its book publishing program.

Giramondo Publishing is assisted by the Australian Government through the Australia Council for the Arts.

HEAT Series 3

Editor Alexandra Christie
Designer Jenny Grigg
Typesetter Andrew Davies
Copy Editor Aleesha Paz
Marketing and Publicity Manager Kate Prendergast
Editorial Intern Lucia Nguyen
Publishers Ivor Indyk and Evelyn Juers
Associate Publisher Nick Tapper

Editorial Advisory Board

Chris Andrews, Mieke Chew, J.M. Coetzee, Lucy Dougan, Lisa Gorton,
Bella Li, Tamara Sampey-Jawad, Suneeta Peres da Costa,
Alexis Wright and Ashleigh Young.

Contact

For editorial enquiries, please email
heat.editor@giramondopublishing.com.
Follow us on Instagram @HEAT.lit and
Twitter @HEAT_journal.

Accessibility

We understand that some formats will not be accessible to all readers.
If you are a reader with specific access requirements, please contact
orders@giramondopublishing.com.

For more information, visit giramondopublishing.com/heat.

Published June 2022
from the Writing and Society Research Centre
at Western Sydney University
by the Giramondo Publishing Company
PO Box 752
Artarmon NSW 1570 Australia
www.giramondopublishing.com

This collection © Giramondo Publishing 2022
Typeset in Tiempos and Founders Grotesk Condensed
designed by Kris Sowersby at Klim Type Foundry

Printed and bound by Ligare Book Printers
Distributed in Australia by NewSouth Books

A catalogue record for this book is available from
the National Library of Australia.

HEAT Series 3 Number 3
ISBN: 978-1-922725-02-8
ISSN: 1326-1460

ISBN 978-1-922725-02-8

9 781922 725028 >